M000282029

Reading Your Future in the Cards
by Eden

ORIGINAL PUBLICATIONS
NEW YORK

Reading Your Future in the Cards
by Eden

Copyright © 2000 Original Publications

ISBN: 0-942272-58-7

All Rights Reserved
No portion of this book may be reproduced in any form
or by any means without written permission from the Publisher.

ORIGINAL PUBLICATIONS
P.O. Box 236
Old Bethpage, New York 11804-0236
1 (888) OCCULT-1

TABLE OF CONTENTS

READING YOUR FUTURE IN THE CARDS

For centuries playing cards have been used as a means of telling fortunes, and many methods of reading their meaning have been developed and passed down from generation to generation. There are presented here some of the more representative systems of the time-honored tradition of card divination.

General Instructions. Among practitioners of fortune telling by cards, or Cartomancy as it is called, it is generally held pat the cards should not be consulted too frequently. Some say that they should not be consulted more often than once a week; it is the opinion of others that they may be read more frequently, but under no circumstances should they be read more than once a day. And no sitting should last more than an hour or two at most.

It is not considered lucky to read the cards alone. Two persons are required for this. The one who wishes to have his fortune told is known as the *Questioner.* The one who assists him by reading the meaning of the cards is referred to in the following pages as the *Seer.*

In cutting the cards the Questioner should always use the left hand.

Before the reading begins the Questioner usually has to select a card which will represent him, and which is known as the Questioner's card. If the Questioner is dark-haired, with dark eyes and dark complexion, the King of Spades is usually chosen to represent a man and the Queen of Spades a woman. The King and Queen of Clubs represent, according to sex, the Questioner who has brown hair and brown eyes. Questioners with blue or gray eyes and light brown hair are represented by the King and Queen of Hearts, according to sex, while with blond Questioners, the Queen of Diamonds represents the women and the King of Diamonds the men.

The Two Major Systems. There are two major systems for using the ordinary pack of bridge or playing cards in fortune telling. One system makes use of the entire deck of fifty-two cards. The other uses only thirty-two cards, the twos, threes, fours, fives and sixes being discarded. Since this later system is usually easier for beginners to master, it is presented first.

THE DECK OF 32 CARDS
- A METHOD FOR BEGINNERS -

After the lower cards, from twos through sixes, have been discarded from the regulation pack, the remaining thirty-two cards must be marked so as to indicate the top and bottom of each card. This may be done by putting a light pencil mark in one corner of each card. In this way the Seer will be able to determine at a glance whether the card has been laid down in normal or reversed position. This is most important, for the meaning of the card depends upon whether it appears reverser or not.

THE MEANING OF THE 32 CARDS

CLUBS

ACE - Good luck. Favorable news, possibly that the Questioner will receive money. A letter.   *Reversed* - *Good* news but the happiness will be brief. The correspondence we not be pleasant.

KING - A dark man, loyal friend, honest.
Reversed - Worry or disappointment, good plans coming to naught.

QUEEN - A dark woman, a friend, full of devotion.
Reversed - unreliable, a flirt, jealous.

JACK - Dark young man, bright and amusing, bold and eager in wooing.
Reversed - He is fickle, a flatterer.

TEN - Good fortune, ease and luxury.
Reversed - A trifling failure, or travel possibly by air or water.

NINE - Unexpected windfall in the way of money.
Reversed - A little gift, or some sort of difficulty.

EIGHT - Love from a worthy individual, bringing fortune and happiness.
Reversed - Unworthy love, bringing trouble. Or papers bringing trouble.

SEVEN - Small money or business affair.
Reversed - Difficulties over money. An unfavorable omen possibly involving legal matters.

HEARTS

ACE - Pleasant tidings, a love letter, the Questioner's home.
Reversed - Change of place, a friend's visit.

KING - Fair-haired man, loyal and friendly.
Reversed - Disappointment connected with this person.

QUEEN - Light-haired woman, dependable and affectionate.
Reversed - Unhappy love connected with her. She may be fickle.

JACK - Fun-loving young bachelor; possibly a child.
Reversed - Young man linked with disappointment or unhappiness, possibly a soldier.

TEN - Very favorable. Good luck, happiness. A proposal. Helps to cancel bad cards.   *Reversed* - Fleeting trouble, possibly a birth.

NINE - This represents the wish. Also slight troubles, but eventual success.   *Reversed* - Fleeting troubles.

EIGHT - Love from a light-complexioned person. Marriage thoughts.
Reversed - Love that is not returned.

SEVEN - Happy thoughts.   *Reversed* - Boredom, possible jealousy.

DIAMONDS

ACE - A letter. Marriage offer.   *Reversed*—News that brings sorrow.

KING - Man with light hair (possibly gray), may be a soldier.
Reversed - Deception or treacherousness, possibly connected with him.

QUEEN - Light-haired woman, rather common and Van gossipy.
Reversed - Difficulties caused by the malice of this woman.

JACK - A young man, an employee, someone in a subordinate position.
Reversed - He causes trouble, cannot be trusted.

TEN - Journey or change of residence.
Reversed - Bad luck as a result of the trip or change of residence.

NINE - Trouble coming, worries, annoyances.
Reversed - Dispute in the family or between lovers.

EIGHT - A love affair.
Reversed - Disappointment in love, affections spurned.

SEVEN - Teasing, unkind criticism, possibly a child.
Reverse - A minor scandal or some small slander.

SPADES

ACE - Satisfaction or pleasure connected with the emotions.
Reversed - Sorrow or sad news.

KING - A dark man, possibly a widower, untrustworthy.
Reversed - A dangerous foe wishing to work evil.

QUEEN - A widow or an older woman.
Reversed - A wit bent upon evil-doing.

JACK - A young man, possibly a student in law or medicine. An ill-bred young fellow.   *Reversed* - A disloyal young man, deceitful and dangerous.

TEN - Misery and sorrow, loss of liberty.
Reversed - The trouble will be of brief duration.

NINE - A bad omen. News of loss or failure.
Reversed - happiness for someone close to the Questioner.

EIGHT - Approaching disappointment.
Reversed - A love affair or match broken up. Impure living.

SEVEN - Anxieties; the making of a new resolution.
Reversed - Silly scheming in love.

MEANING OF CARD GROUPS

4 ACES - Perils, loss of money or honor, separations. If, ace is reversed, these troubles are not so grave; if two are reversed, the danger is further lessened; if they are all reversed, it is slight.

3 ACES - Brief anxieties, with good tidings to follow, if all are reversed they foretell a foolhardy action.

2 ACES - Some sort of partnership; the diamond and spade together indicate evil or misfortune to come. Other combinations are favorable. If one of the cards is reversed, the partnership will not be entirely successful. If both are reversed, it will fail.

4 KINGS - Advancement, wealth, honor. With each reversed card, the good fortune will be less but it will happen sooner.

3 KINGS - Something of great importance is to be started the more cards that are reversed, the less successful it will be.

2 KINGS - A commercial alliance. One reversed means partial success. Both reversed mean failure.

4 QUEENS - A social affair. The more cards that are reversed, the more the fun will be spoiled by unexpected circumstances.

3 QUEENS - A gathering of friends. With each reversed card there is greater danger of scandal-mongering and trouble.

2 QUEENS - A talk between friends, with secrets given away. One reversed indicates rivals. Both reversed means trouble for the one who learns the secret.

4 JACKS - A hilarious party. The more cards that are reversed, the wilder the hilarity, with possible trouble as an outcome.

3 JACKS - Trouble among friends, possibly from gossip. With each reversed card there is greater danger of a quarrel leading to blows.

2 JACKS - Loss of some sort, possibly theft. One reversed means the loss will not happen right away. Both reversed mean it will happen very soon.

4 TENS - Exceptionally good luck in store, especially regarding the Questioner's present undertakings.   *Reversed* - The more cards that are reversed, the more hazards that must be overcome before success is reached.

3 TENS - Failure and trouble through legal proceedings. With each reversed card the trouble become less serious.

2 TENS - A lucky break coming without warning, it may involve a new kind of occupation. One reversed means it will take place very shortly. Both reversed mean some time will elapse before it occurs.

4 NINES - Unexpected occurrences. The more cards that are reversed, the sooner the surprise will come.

3 NINES - A most favorable sign. Increased prosperity, good health, enjoyment of life. Each reversed card represents an additional amount of brief worry and care before the good fortune occurs.

2 NINES - Some sort of success in commercial affairs. If one or both are reversed, this indicates small troubles and anxiety.

4 EIGHTS - New kind of occupation or small trip. The more cards that are reversed, the sooner this will occur.

3 EIGHTS - The Questioner's thoughts regarding marriage and love. If any one is reversed, it means merely a flirtation.

2 EIGHTS - A short love affair. One reversed means a disappointment in connection with love. Both reversed mean a sadness resulting from the Questioner's previous actions.

4 SEVENS - Foes working in secret against the Questioner. The more cards that are reversed, the more likely their plottings will fail and they will be suitably punished.

3 SEVENS - Unhappiness, or the loss of friends. With each reversed card the unhappiness will be less severe.

2 SEVENS - Love that is reciprocated. One reversed means deception in love. Both reversed mean regrets over love.

MEANING OF SPECIAL COMBINATIONS
WITH 32 CARDS

In addition to the above meanings of the individual cards and the groups of the same denomination there are also certain combinations of two or more cards which have special meanings when the pack of 32 cards is used. These are listed below according to the four suits for rapid identification. It should be understood that these meanings apply *only* when the cards listed appear *side by side*.

CLUBS

ACE - When surrounded by *diamonds* or with diamonds not more than one card away from it, the Ace of Clubs signifies money coming to the Questioner. With the *nine of diamonds* it indicates legal business of some sort.

KING - With *ten of clubs*, an offer of marriage is to be expected.

QUEEN - With *seven of diamonds* this Queen indicates an uncertain outcome of events. With *Ace of Spades*, a tiresome journey.

JACK - With *Jack of Spades*, loss of money, unprofitable business ventures.

TEN - With *Ace* of any suit following this indicates a big amount of cash.

NINE - With ten of hearts this indicates the stage or screen, possibly a theater. With *nine of hearts* it foretells a will or legacy bringing good fortune to the Questioner. With *eight of hearts* it indicates a good time or celebration.

EIGHT - With Ace of Diamonds, money coming unexpectedly. With *ten of diamonds*, a trip in connection with a love affair. With *eight of diamonds*, true love.

SEVEN - With *Jack of Hearts*, a love affair in which one party is more interested in gaining social prestige or financial advantage than in true and unselfish devotion. With *ten of spades*, an omen of misfortune in the future.

HEARTS

ACE – When surrounded by *hearts* or with hearts not more than one card away from it, this indicates the beloved, or domestic buss.

KING – With *nine of hearts*, a love affair with a happy future.

QUEEN – With *seven of diamonds*, joy coming unexpectedly. With *ten of spades*, a dangerous undertaking.

JACK – With *seven of clubs*, a love affair where one party is motivated by a selfish interest in gaining social prestige or financial advantage.

TEN – With *ten of diamonds*, a marriage ceremony. With *nine of clubs*, the stage or screen, possibly the theater.

NINE – With *nine of clubs*, a will or legacy bringing good fortune to the Questioner.

EIGHT – With *nine of diamonds*, travel to some distant place.
With *eight of diamonds*, the beginning of new and important work. With *nine of clubs*, a good time or celebration.

SEVEN – With *Queen of Diamonds*, happiness overshadowed by jealousy.

DIAMONDS

ACE – When surrounded by *diamonds* this indicates the Questioner will prosper financially in his present occupation. With the *eight of clubs*, money coming unexpectedly. With the *seven and Jack of Diamonds*, a telegram or wireless message.

KING – With *eight of spades*, a sudden journey.

QUEEN – With *seven of spades*, success to be found in a small community rather than in a large city.

JACK – With *Ace* and *seven of diamonds*, see Ace of Diamonds.

TEN – With *ten of hearts*, a marriage ceremony. With *eight of clubs*, a trip in connection with a love affair. With *seven of spades*, a lapse of time caused by a delay.

NINE – With *Ace of Clubs*, legal business of some sort. With *eight of hearts*, travel to some distant place.

EIGHT – With *eight of clubs*, true love. With *eight of hearts*, the beginning of new and important work.

SEVEN - With *Ace* and *Jack of Diamonds*, see Ace of Diamonds. With *eight of spades*, the need to ask for help. With *Queen of Clubs*, an uncertain outcome of events. With *Queen of Hearts*, joy coming unexpectedly.

SPADES

ACE - With *Queen of Clubs*, a tiresome journey.

KING - With *seven of clubs*, caution necessary in connection with investments.

QUEEN - With *Jack of Spades*, the Queen signifies a woman of most evil intentions.

JACK - See Queen of Spades.

TEN - With *Queen of Hearts*, an exciting venture.

NINE - With *Jack of Diamonds*, the advice of friends should not be accepted too readily.

EIGHT - With *King of Diamonds*, a sudden journey. With *seven of diamonds*, the need to ask for help.

SEVEN - With *ten of diamonds*, a lapse of time caused by a delay. With the *King, Queen* or *Jack of Spades*, this indicates a traitor posing as a loyal supporter.

MISCELLANEOUS

When a *heart* card of any sort follows a King or Queen of any one of the suits, that King or Queen represents someone who wants to be a close friend of or in love with the Questioner.

If a King, Queen or Jack has cards of the same number on either side (as *eight, Jack, eight,* or *Ace, King, Ace*), it is a sign of caution to the person for whom the King, Queen or Jack stands.

When the Ace, King, Queen and Jack of one color fall in that order, a wedding is indicated. If the *seven of clubs is* not more than two cards away from this sequence, the couple will have to face financial problems.

A number of *spades* in a row is a sign of misfortune.

A number of *hearts* in a row is a sign of more than one love match, also social gatherings and domestic joys.

A number of *clubs* in a row is a sign of success and happiness.

A number of *diamonds* in a row is a sign of money transactions, usually to the benefit of the Questioner.

AN OLD FAVORITE

Here is a very old and reliable method. The Questioner shuffles the thirty-two-card pack thoroughly, then cuts them, with the left hand into two sections. From the upper section the Seer removes the bottom card and from the lower section he removes the top card. These two cards he puts aside, face down. They are known as the Surprise.

The Seer then places the lower section on top of the upper section. From this pack of thirty cards he deals off three piles of ten cards each, starting from the right and dealing to the left.

The pile on the left is known as the Past; the pile in the center is the Present; and the pile on the right is the Future.

The Seer now deals out the ten cards of the Past in a row from left to right, and proceeds to read them. He then does the same with the pile of the Present and the pile of the Future. Last he turns over the two cards of the Surprise. They represent a sudden turn of affairs which will have a direct bearing on the future success and happiness of the Questioner.

A Model. Here is a model deal to show how the cards **may** be read. The cards are shuffled and cut by the Questioner, a young woman represented by the Queen of Hearts. The See, having dealt off the cards as directed, the pile of the Past is found to contain the following, reading in order from left to right:

Seven of clubs
King of hearts
Nine of clubs
Ten of clubs
Ace of hearts reversed
Eight of spades reversed
Jack of diamonds
Queen of spades reversed
Ten of spades reversed
Jack of clubs

First we consider the card groups. Two jacks refer to some loss which the Questioner has sustained. The two tens indicate lucky turn of events which came unexpectedly. Looking for special combinations, we find the ten of clubs followed by the Ace of hearts which refers to a large sum of money.

Now taking the cards in order we find the Questioner connected with some small affair having to do with business (seven of clubs) in which she was associated with a loyal and friendly light-haired man (king of hearts) and as a result of which she received an unexpected sum of money (nine of clubs). This apparently was the lucky turn of events indicated by the two tens and involved quite a large sum, as previously shown by the ten clubs / ace of hearts combination, for she was enabled to enjoy ease and luxury (ten of clubs) and to change her place of residence (ace of hearts reversed). We also find the breakup of a romance (eight of spades reversed) in which the Questioner's interests were centered upon a young employee in some business firm (jack of diamonds). This may be the loss of which the pair of jacks speaks, and it was brought about by the interference of a woman who was bent on evil doing (queen of spades reversed). However the Questioner's heartache was of not very great duration (ten of spades reversed), for it is apparent that she soon transferred her affections and found a new interest in a dashing young man, who was both an amusing and witty companion and devoted swain (jack of clubs).

Now turning to the pile of the Present, we find the cards read from left to right in order as follows:

Jack of spades
Eight of hearts
Nine of diamonds
Nine of spades
Queen of clubs reversed
Queen of hearts reversed
Eight of diamonds reversed
Ace of clubs
King of diamonds
Nine of hearts

.Looking for card groups, we find first three nines which is a very favorable sign and indicates increasing prosperity and good health. This is tempered a bit, however, by the presence of the two eights, one of them reversed, which speaks of an appointment in love, a sign which must not be overlooked especially in view of the two queens, both of which are reversed, indicating a talk between friends with secrets being confided and trouble for the one who has learned the secret. The ace of clubs surrounded by diamonds as it refers to money which is coming to the Questioner and the eight of hearts with the nine of diamonds indicates a journey to a distant place.

Now let us study the cards in sequence. We find the young man whom the Questioner is interested in at present. It may possibly be the amusing young fellow whom we found in her Past, and now we learn more about him, for he appears to be a student (jack of spades). It is clear that he is definitely interested in the Questioner, for we see that he is entertaining thoughts of marriage in connection with her (eight of hearts) but unfortunately nothing can be expected to come of this for we see that there is unhappiness ahead (nine of diamonds and nine of spades). We do not look far for the cause, either. It is a jealous flirt (queen of clubs reversed) who is going to steal his heart away. Any doubts we might have about this turn of events is removed by examining the next two cards. We find the Questioner's card (queen of hearts) which is in reversed position, meaning unhappiness in love, and as double proof the eight of diamonds reversed is linked with it, indicating disappointment in love. The disappointment is easily discerning The jealous flirt is doubtlessly a close friend of the Questioner, for we find their cards side by side. Now the significance of the pair of queens previously noted becomes plain. Here are two girl friends having a supposedly friendly talk, with an exchange of confidences, and the Questioner learns to her sorrow that her trusted friend has proved disloyal and stolen the love of the Questioner's young man. Here is unhappiness in love, disappointment in and loss of a friend through love. The ominous warning contained in the nine of spades is indeed bearing fruit. The last three cards speak of other matters. We find a letter bearing good news (ace of clubs) and coming from an elderly, gray-haired man, probably an uncle or a grandfather (king of diamonds). It may be that this letter contains the money which we saw was coming to the Questioner, for it is through the letter that the Questioner obtains her wish (nine of hearts). This checks with the previous favorable indications found in the three nines, and it is possible that the wish may have something to do with travel to a distant place (which has already been noted). The money would provide the means for the realization of this desire and thus would allow the Questioner to enjoy a change of scene and a chance to forget the unhappiness of her friend's betrayal and her shattered romance.

The pile of the Future contains the following cards, from left to right:

*Seven of spades - Queen of diamonds reversed - Seven of diamonds
King of spades reversed - King of clubs reversed - Ten of diamonds
Seven of hearts - Ace of spades - Jack of hearts - Eight of clubs*

We first note two groups of cards with unfavorable meanings. The pair of kings, both reversed, speak of some sort of failure in a commercial enterprise or undertaking. The three sevens speak of great unhappiness. On the basis of the Past and Present it is possible to hazard a guess that these groupings signify that the Questioner's attempt to forget her unhappy love affair by concentrating on a business career is not going to be successful. But we must consult the individual cards first before we draw any final conclusions.

The seven of spades foretells anxiety and worry on the part of the Questioner, caused by the malice of a rather common and vulgar woman (queen of diamonds reversed). In addition we find unkind criticism (seven of diamonds) coming from a man who is an enemy of the Questioner (king of spades reversed) which will lead ultimately to the defeat of the Questioner's best plans (king of clubs reversed). When these predictions are considered in the light of the meaning of the pair of kings, they offer the picture of the Questioner, earnestly trying to make her way in business, being thwarted by a malicious woman, possibly someone who works with her, and by an employer who dislikes her and is constantly criticizing her. In the end her dreams of a career will be spoiled and she will be most unhappy. However beyond this gloomy period of trial and unhappiness we find a much different set of circumstances. A change of residence (ten of diamonds) will bring to a close the unpleasant chapter of the future and will usher in a period of happy thoughts (seven of hearts) and much emotional pleasure and satisfaction (ace of spades). And it is not hard to discern the cause for this sudden change for the better. It is a fun-loving young bachelor (jack of hearts) who is offering a worthy love that is destined to bring fortune and happiness (eight of clubs).

Last we consult the Surprise, where we find a proposal marriage (ace of diamonds) linked with assurance of good and happiness (ten of hearts).

THE SECRET OF THE SEVENS

The Questioner takes the pack of thirty-two cards and after shuffling them well cuts them into three sections. The Seer takes the section on the Questioner's right and places it on top of the section on the Questioner's left. The center section now placed on top of these two.

Now the Seer proceeds to deal out the cards, right to left and face up, in four rows of seven cards each, with a fifth row of four cards.

Each row is considered as containing some message in regard to the future. The Seer first reads the meanings of the cards in the top row, proceeding from left to right in order to find out the message or prediction contained in the row. He then consults the second row, and so on until he has covered all five rows.

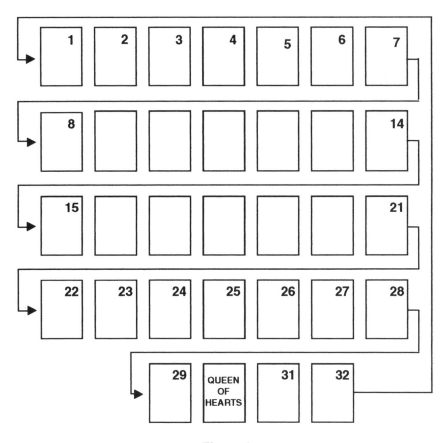

Figure 1

13

Now the Seer locates the Questioner's card, the choice of which is explained in the *General Instructions* at the beginning of the chapter, and counts off seven from it in either direction. The two cards thus located (the seventh on the right and the seventh on the left of the Questioner's card) are read together as a special forecast relating to the Questioner himself. It should be explained at this point that in order to be able to count off seven in either direction, it is necessary to regard the five rows of cards as being in reality a continuous chain. *Figure I* illustrates how this works. Card 7 at the end of the top row is considered to lie next to Card 8 at the beginning of the second row, and so on. Likewise the last card in the bottom row, 32, leads directly back to Card I at the beginning of the top row. Thus in counting off seven in either direction from the queen of hearts in the bottom row we arrive at Card 5 in the top row and Card 23 in the fourth row.

The Seer also locates the nine of hearts (wish card) and counts off seven in each direction to find the message concerning the Questioner's wish. Similarly he reads the message connected with the Questioner's home (ace of hearts), with the letter the Questioner is about to receive (ace of clubs), and with the Questioner's current love affair (eight of diamonds).

A Model. Here is a model reading of this interesting method. The cards are shuffled and cut by the Questioner, who is a man represented by the king of diamonds. The Seer deals off the cards in the five rows as directed. Examining the first or top, row for its message, he finds these cards in the following order from left to right:

> *Ace of hearts*
> *King of diamonds*
> *Queen of hearts*
> *Ace of spades reversed*
> *Jack of diamonds reversed*
> *Seven of diamonds reversed*
> *Eight of spades reversed*

Looking for groups we find a pair of aces, one reversed, which indicate some sort of partnership which will be only partly successful. In special combinations to be noted there is the queen of hearts which appears with the ace of hearts, the sign of the beloved. In this case reference is obviously made to the woman with whom the king of diamonds (Questioner) is in love. The seven of diamonds with the eight of spades foretells the necessity for asking for help. A study of the cards individually should make these points clearer.

First we find a love letter (ace of hearts) coming to the Questioner (king of diamonds) from a dependable and affectionate woman, with light complexion and fair hair (queen of hearts). It is evident that this woman's sentiments are returned, for we have already noted the special combination referring to beloved. Consequently the king of diamonds and the queen hearts must represent the partnership - one of affection rather than commerce, in this case - of which the pair of aces spoke and we have been warned that this partnership will not be altogether successful. We do not have to look far to find this prediction borne out. Next to the Questioner's card we find ace of spades reversed, which indicates unhappiness and discord. This is evidently because the letter was delivered by a young man who could not be trusted (jack of diamonds reversed) and who used his knowledge of the contents of the message to create a scandal (seven of diamonds reversed). The outcome of this unfortunate situation is the breaking off of the love affair (eight of spades).

In the second row we find the following cards, left to right:

Seven of clubs reversed
King of spades reversed
Jack of spades reversed
Ace of clubs reversed
Ten of clubs reversed
Seven of spades
Nine of clubs

In this row we find a pair of sevens, one of them reversed, which indicates deception in love. As there are no special combinations here we can proceed at once to examine the cards individually.

There is at the outset a warning to the Questioner of money troubles (seven of clubs reversed) which are to come, and since these are brought on by the scheming of an unscrupulous man (king of spades reversed) it is probable that this enemy is a rival of the Questioner's in love, having also instigated the aforementioned deception. We find that this enemy is assisted in his evil doing by a deceitful and dangerous young man (jack of spades reversed) and as a result of their combined efforts a most unpleasant correspondence is going to ensue (ace of clubs reversed) which eventually will end in making it necessary for the Questioner to make a journey (ten of clubs reversed) which will be very unpleasant and filled with anxieties (seven of spades). However in the end all will turn out for the best, for the Questioner will, as a result of his journey, come into possession of an unexpected sum of money (nine of clubs).

The message of the third row is contained in the following cards, reading from left to right:

Queen of spades
Queen of clubs reversed
Seven of hearts reversed
Nine of spades
King of hearts
Ten of hearts
Nine of hearts

Looking for groups, we find a pair of queens, one of them reversed, which tells us of a rivalry. The pair of nines speaks of success in commercial affairs.

It is evident that this message concerns the Questioner's business dealings. We see him associated in commerce with two women, one an older type (queen of spades) and the other a vamp (queen of clubs reversed). These women find themselves rivals for his interest, and though there is no evidence that the Questioner entertains any special feelings toward either of them, it is obvious that the philanderer's interest in him is not solely confined to business, for there is an indication of jealousy (seven of hearts reversed) at work. This situation is going to lead to trouble the Questioner will suffer some sort of loss as a result (nine of spades). However, through the intercession of a loyal and trusted friend (king of hearts) matters will soon be straightened out and everything will turn out for the best (ten of hearts) and the Questioner will realize the success in his commercial affairs which the pair of nines suggested, for we see that his wish will be granted (nine of hearts). The message of the fourth row is contained in these cards, reading from left to right:

Eight of hearts
Ten of diamonds
Jack of clubs
Nine of diamonds
King of clubs reversed
Eight of clubs
Ace of diamonds

Studying the row for groups, we find a pair of eights, which indicate a short love affair. In the special combinations we discover the eight of clubs with the ace of diamonds, a welcome sign foretelling the receipt of an unexpected sum of money.

At the outset we find the Questioner entertaining thoughts of marriage (eight of hearts) which are interrupted when he is compelled to make a journey (ten of diamonds) in the company of a bright and amusing young man (jack of clubs). The journey, however, brings trouble and worry (nine of diamonds) and the Questioner sees his well-laid plans coming to naught (King of clubs reversed). But despite this misfortune his love is returned by a worthy individual (eight of clubs) and we find the brief courtship forecast in the pair of eights terminated by a proposal of marriage (ace of diamonds), which we may assume is accepted, since the eight of clubs, indicates a love which will result in good fortune in happiness.

In the last row of four cards we find the following cards, reading from left to right:

Jack of hearts
Eight of diamonds reversed
Ten of spades reversed
Queen of diamonds

This message appears to be a warning to a friend of the Questioner, a happy-go-lucky young bachelor (jack of hearts) who is going to suffer a disappointment in a love affair (eight of diamonds reversed) and a certain amount of misery and unhappiness (ten of spades reversed) because of the idle chatter and talebearing of a gossipy woman (queen of diamonds) The unhappiness will fortunately not last very long, as is shown by the position of the ten of spades, which is reversed.

Finally we turn to the individual cards relating to the Questioner, his wish, his home, etc., and look for the special messages of the sevens in regard to them.

Counting off seven in each direction from the Questioner's card (king of diamonds) as previously described, we arrive at the eight of clubs and the king of spades reversed. This is a message informing the Questioner that in a love affair with a worthy individual (eight of clubs) he must beware the influence of a dangerous enemy who will seek to wreck his happiness (king of spades reversed).

Regarding the Questioner's wish, we count off seven from the nine of hearts and obtain the following message: The wish will be granted as a result of a letter (ace of diamonds) which will contain an unexpected sum of money (nine of clubs).

Concerning the letter (ace of clubs) he is going to receive, the count of sevens reveals that it will contain unpleasant news.

Regarding his present love affair (eight of diamonds) the count of sevens predicts that there is going to be interference in the Questioner's romance by a young man who is a troublemaker (jack of diamonds reversed) and that the Questioner is going to have to make a journey (ten of diamonds) in order to patch things up.

THE FATEFUL ELEVEN

The Questioner takes the pack of cards and shuffles it thoroughly. It is then cut into three piles. The Seer places the center pile on the one on the left, and these two together are placed upon the remaining pile, which was the one on the right.

The Seer now turns the pack face up and, picking off the three uppermost cards, chooses the one which ranks highest, regardless of suit. In case two of the three cards are alike (or all three are alike), choice of high card is made by considering clubs highest, then hearts, then diamonds and last spades. (It should be remembered that in this method the ace ranks above the king.)

Having chosen the highest of the three top cards, the Seer places it face up on the table and discards its two companions face down. Now the Seer picks off the next three cards of the pack and again selects the one of highest rank, placing it face up to the left of the previously chosen high card and discarding its two companions. This process continues, each selected high card always being laid down in the row to the left of the preceding one, until the entire pack has been exhausted. At the end two cards will remain instead of three. Of these last two the Seer chooses the one having the lower value and places it last in the row of selected cards. Its partner goes into the discard pile.

There are now eleven cards face up in the row on the table and twenty-one face down in the discard heap. These latter twenty-one are now carefully shuffled by the Questioner and handed to the Seer who proceeds to deal them out face up in two rows, one of eleven cards and the other of ten. The cards in these two rows are now read, each row carrying a message for the Questioner. Finally the original row of eleven selected cards is read for its message, certain portents being carefully posed. If the nine of hearts (wish card), the ten of hearts or ace of clubs happens to be in this row, it is an exceptionally favorable sign regarding the Questioner's future and helps to cancel the effects of any evil combinations. If the nine of spades is in this row, however, it is a warning to the Questioner to proceed with extreme caution in everything he does for the next two weeks or so.

In reading the cards the Seer must always remember to look first for groups and special combinations before proceeding to interpret the significance of the cards individually.

THE DOUBLE THIRTEEN

The Questioner shuffles the pack thoroughly and hands it the Seer, who deals the cards out into two piles. With the hand the Questioner now cuts the pile on his right, taking care not to look at the cut card. This the Seer removes, also taking care not to look at it, and places to one side face down as of the Surprise. The Questioner then cuts the other pile in the same manner, and the Seer removes the cut card and places it face down with the first one as the second half of the Surprise

The remaining thirty cards are now shuffled again by Questioner and cut into two piles, from which the Seer moves the top and bottom card of each and discards them. The two piles are placed together again and reshuffled by the Questioner. The Seer then takes the pack and deals out two rows of thirteen cards each, face up. The message which each of these contains for the Questioner is now read, the Seer taking care first to note all groups and special combinations.

When this has been done the Questioner examines both rows and chooses a card to represent himself or herself, as case may be. In this method any king may be selected to represent a man and any queen a woman.

Once the Questioner's card has been decided on, the twenty- six cards are gathered together and reshuffled by the Questioner. The Seer now takes the pack and deals out two rows nine and one row of eight, right to left and face up. The Questioner's card is now located in one of these rows. The other two rows may then be ignored. The Seer studies the six cards nearest to the Questioner's card for any message which they may contain. These six will be the three to the right of the

Questioner's card and the three to its left. If the Questioner's placed so near the end of the row that there are not three cards on either side, then there will be less than six cards to consider. In Fig. 2 this situation is illustrated. The Questioner's card (Q) is shown third from the left end of a row of nine. The shaded cards represent those which contain the special message. Three of these appear on the right of the Questioner's card, but there are only two to the left of it. Consequently only these two, plus the three on the right may be considered. In like manner, if the Questioner's card had appeared as the last card at the right end of the row, only the three cards marked A, B and C could have been considered for the special message.

After this reading has been completed, the Seer turns up the two cards in the Surprise and determines what unexpected event is going to affect the future success and happiness of the Questioner.

Figure 2

THE SINGLE THIRTEEN

The Questioner selects the card which is to represent him according to the directions given under the heading *General Instructions*. This card is laid up in the center of the table. The remaining thirty-one are now shuffled by the Questioner and handed to the Seer, who deals off thirteen face down. This thirteenth card is placed face up on the table to the *right* of the Questioner's card. The Seer cuts the cards which remain in his hand and places the cut card face up on the table to the *left* of the Questioner's card. The cards are now shuffled again by the Questioner and the Seer deals off eleven, placing the eleventh face up *above* the Questioner's card. The cards remaining in the Seer's hand are cut and the cut card is placed face up *beneath* the Questioner's card.

This process is continued until the layout shown in Figure 3 in is built up. The numbers indicate the order in which the are placed about the Questioner's card. Each time after the Seer has placed the cut card, the rest of the pack is reshuffled by the Questioner.

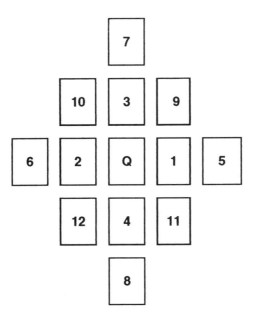

Figure 3

It should be noted that the Seer first deals off thirteen cards, placing the thirteenth in the layout. On the next deal he deals only eleven cards, placing the eleventh card in the position bearing the number 3 in the diagram. The third time he deals off, he deals only nine cards, the ninth being placed in position No. 5 as indicated in Fig. 3. (The cut card after this deal goes in position number 6.) On the fourth deal only seven are dealt off. On the fifth deal only five are dealt and on the sixth and last only three are dealt from the pack, the third going in position No. 11. The cards remaining in the Seer's hand are then cut for the last time, with the cut card going in position No. 12.

The layout is now complete and the reading may start. The Seer begins with the top card (position No. 7), considering how it is related to the Questioner in connection with the card beneath it (position No. 3). The cards in positions 10, 3 and 9 are considered as a group, since they adjoin one another. Likewise positions 10, 2 and 12 are studied together for related meanings. The same naturally applies to positions 9, 1 and 11, 12, 4 and 11.

Though this is not one of the easiest methods, its adherents claim great things for it, insisting that it can reveal much that lies in the mysterious future.

THE FIFTEEN-SEVEN METHOD

This is an old peasant method, which is said to produce remarkably accurate forecasts of things to come. The Questioner selects a card to represent him according to the directions given under the heading *General Instructions*. This card is placed face up on the table. He then shuffles the remaining thirty-one cards and hands the pack to the Seer.

Placing the pack face down on the table, the Seer proceeds to turn over three cards at a time. If two are of the suit he takes the one with the highest value and places it face down to the left of the Questioner's card. If they are all of the suit, he lays the three face down and in order next to the Questioner's card, starting on the left. If none of the cards are of the same suit, he discards them. Three more cards are turned up from the pack and the same process of selection and rejection is repeated. This continues until a row of fourteen cards has been built up from the left of the Questioner's card. If after the entire pack has been dealt out in this way there are not fourteen cards next to the Questioner's, the discarded cards must be reshuffled by the Questioner and the Seer must over again, dealing off three at a time.

When the fourteen cards have finally been chosen and placed in a row face down beside the Questioner's card, the row is bent around to form a circle, care being taken so as not to disturb the order in which the cards lie. Starting with the Questioner's card, the Seer now counts off seven around the circle. The counting may be done in either direction. The seventh is removed from the circle and placed by itself face up. The card which was next to this one now becomes the starting point for a new count, and continuing around the circle in same direction, the Seer counts off seven again, removing the seventh card and placing it face up to the left of its predecessor. The count continues by sevens, proceeding around the dwindling circle until all the cards have been counted off and placed in a row face up from right to left.

The message of this row is now read, the Seer paying special heed to groups and special combinations. When this has been done, the Seer picks up the two end cards of the row, places them together and notes their combined meaning. The two cards which now appear at the end of the shortened row are likewise picked up, placed together and "read." This is continued until only three cards remain in the row. These three are considered together for any special meaning they may have.

Next the fifteen cards are reshuffled and dealt out into three piles, each pile then being studied separately for its special message.

Finally the fifteen cards are reshuffled and dealt out as follows: three piles of four cards each, which are known respectively as *The Questioner, The Questioner's Beloved* and *The Questioner's Home*. The three remaining cards are dealt out in a row and the middle one is laid aside as the *Surprise*. The remaining cards are put together as *the wish*. The three piles are then read in order for the messages which they contain. The message of the first obviously refers to the Questioner, of the second to his sweetheart, etc. The message regarding his Wish is read next, and last the Surprise.

THE STAR OF SEVENTEEN

The Questioner first chooses a card to represent him according to the directions given under the heading *General Instructions*. This card is placed in center of the table face up and the remaining thirty-one are carefully shuffled by the Questioner.

The Seer takes the pack and deals off the first eleven cards, which are discarded. The Questioner reshuffles the remaining and cuts them into two piles. The Seer removes the top and bottom card of each pile and discards them. The cards which now remain are again shuffled by the Questioner and handed to the Seer.

The Seer begins to deal them off, laying them around the Questioner's card in the order which is indicated by the numbers in Figure 4. (The shaded cards in the diagram, marked 17, 18,19 and 20, should be disregarded for the present.) Thus the first card dealt off is laid sideways to the right of the Questioner's card; the second sideways to the left of the Questioner's card; the third vertically above the Questioner's card, etc.

Once the seventeen-card star has been laid out, the Seer proceeds to read the cards in pairs, relating the message of each pair to the Questioner. The pairs are read in order as follows: 1 with 2, 3 with 4, 5 with 9, 6 with 10, 7 with 11, 8 with 12, 13 with 15, and 14 with 16. The nearer a pair is to the Questioner's card, the more immediate will be the results predicted in its message, though this is not a hard and fast rule. Nearness to the Questioner's card depends largely upon the order in which the cards are read. Thus the message of cards 1 and 2 has immediate significance, while that of cards 14 and 16 refer to some event that will not take place until after a certain lapse of time.

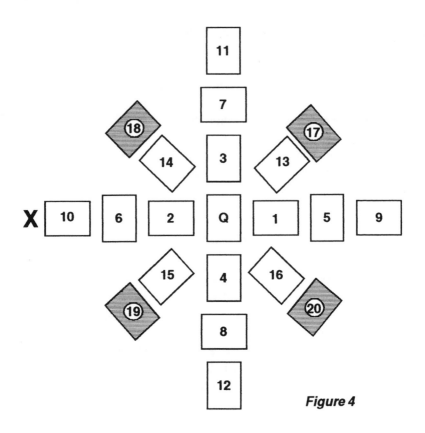

Figure 4

It should be noted that from the observer's point of view (which is the Seer's) in Fig. 4, the cards numbered 1, 2, 7, 8, 9 and 10 are lying sideways, thus making it difficult to determine whether they are in reversed or normal position. To ascertain it is necessary for the Seer to move around to the left side of the layout (at the point marked X in the diagram) in order to properly study these particular cards. After noting their values from this position, he can resume his seat and proceed the reading.

A Variation. A variation of the Star of Seventeen is the Star of Twenty-One, which is preferred by some Seers, since it gives evidence about the future of the Questioner. The Star of Twenty-One is laid out in precisely the same manner in which Star of Seventeen is formed, with these exceptions:

24

Instead of dealing off and discarding eleven cards at the outset, the Seer deals off and discards only seven. The remaining cards are reshuffled by the Questioner and cut as before, with the top and bottom cards of the two piles being removed. After the final shuffle by the Questioner, the Seer lays them out in the same manner as previously indicated. The extra cards which remain after the sixteenth has been dealt are placed in the positions 17, 18, 19 and 20 as indicated by the four shaded cards in Fig.4. These last four cards are also read in pairs, 17 with 19 and 18 with 20.

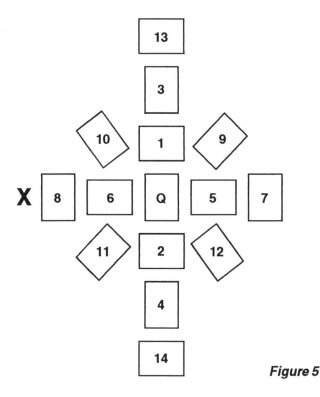

Figure 5

THE LUCKY STAR

Another favorite pattern based on the star employs only a total of fifteen cards. The Questioner's card is first selected according to the rules given under the heading *General Instructions*. This is placed face up in the center of the table and the Questioner shuffles the remaining thirty-one cards and then cuts them into three piles of approximately equal size.

25

The Seer now starts to build up the star. Taking the top card off the center pile, he places it face up and sideways above Questioner's card. The top card of the right-hand pile is placed face up and sideways beneath the Questioner's card. The top card of the left-hand pile is next placed face up and sideways to the right of the Questioner's card. In Fig. 5 the positions of the cards as they are drawn and laid out are indicated. The Seer continues drawing cards off the three piles in the same order: center pile, then right-hand, then left hand. After the fourteenth card has been placed as indicated the rest of the cards are discarded and the reading begins by pairs as was explained under the *Star of Seventeen*. The order in which the pairs are read is as follows: first 1 with 3, then 2 with 4, 5 with 7, 6 with 8, 9 with 11, 10 with 12, and 13 with 14.

As in the case of the *Star of Seventeen*, some of the cards lie sideways. In order to determine whether they are in reversed or normal position, the Seer must move around to the left side of the layout (at the point marked X in Fig. 5) in order properly to study these cards, which are 1, 2, 5, 6, 13 and 14.

Special note must be taken of the message of the last two cards - 13 and 14. In the *Lucky Star* method these last two are said to foretell something which is to occur in the very near future. In other respects the reading of the cards differs very slightly from that of the *Star of Seventeen*.

THE SIMPLE CROSS

First the Questioner selects a card to represent himself according to the directions given under the heading *General Instructions*. This is laid face up on the table and the remaining thirty-one cards are carefully shuffled and cut by the Questioner into two approximately piles. From each of these the Seer removes the top and bottom cards and discards them.

The Questioner reshuffles the remaining cards and deals out four packs of six cards each. Three cards remain in the Questioner's hand and these he discards. The four packs are now together again and shuffled by the Questioner and handed to the Seer.

The Seer deals off the first four cards and adds them to the discard pile. He now takes the remaining cards and turns them face up. The first one he places to the right of the Questioner's card; the second goes to the left of the Questioner's card; the third goes above the Questioner's card, and the fourth below it. The fifth is laid on top of the Questioner's card. The sixth placed on top of the first (at the right of the Questioner's card); the seventh on top of the second, etc., the process is continued until all the cards have been laid out. There is now a pile of four cards to the right, the left, above, and below ,Questioner's card, as well as four cards on top of it. In Fig. 6 the order is indicated in which the cards are laid out in piles. Thus in the pile on the right are to be found cards 1, 6, 11 and 16, while piled on top of the Questioner's card are those numbered 5, 10, 15 and 20, etc.

The Seer now begins the reading. First he considers the message to be found in the pile of four cards to the left of the Questioner's card, and then the message in the pile below the Questioner's card. These two refer to the Questioner's past. The pile to the right of the Questioner's card is considered next and then the one above it, these two referring to the Questioner's future. Last the Seer studies the four cards which lie on top of the Questioner's card. Their message relates to Questioner's wish

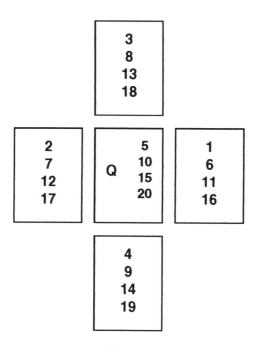

Figure 6

THE GYPSY CROSS

This method of card divination requires a second-pack of fifty-two cards in addition to the marked pack of thirty-two. From the pack of fifty-two an ace, two, three, four and five any suit are removed and placed face down in a row on the table.

The Questioner now chooses from the marked pack of thirty-two cards one which will represent him. This is done according to the rules given under the heading *General Instructions*. This card is placed face up in the center of the table.

The remaining thirty-one cards are now shuffled carefully, by the Questioner and cut with the left hand. The Seer now takes the pack and holding it face down lays the top card beneath the Questioner's card. The next card is placed to the right of the Questioner's card, the third card goes above the Questioner's card, the fourth card is placed to the left of it, and the fifth card placed on top of it.

The Seer then deals off seven cards and discards them. He then adds five more cards from the pack to the five which have already been laid down about the Questioner's card, following the same order as before—first below, then to the right, then above, then left and last on top of the Questioner's card.

Once more he deals off seven cards and discards them, and then he adds the next five cards to the ones already laid down, again in the same order as previously given. After this the two remaining cards in his hand are discarded.

There are now three cards in a pile above, below, on the right and on the left of the Questioner's card, and three on top of it. In Fig. 7 the order is indicated in which the cards are laid out in the five piles.

The Questioner now turns to the five cards from the full pack of fifty-two which were laid face down on the table at the beginning. Shuffling them so that he has no idea of their identity, he selects one and places it on the pile of cards below the Questioner's card, turning it face up as he does so. He then picks another of the four remaining cards and lays it on the pile at the right of the Questioner's card, turning it face up as does so. This is repeated with the three remaining cards, they being placed in order upon the pile above the Questioner's card, upon the one to the left of it and lastly on top of it.

With these five cards - ace, two, three, four and five - lying face up, the Seer is now able to determine the order in which he will read the messages of the five piles. The pile on which the ace is lying is read first, the ace is not considered to be part of the message but merely an indicator of the order in which the reading shall proceed. Next the cards which lie under the two are read, then those under the three, etc.

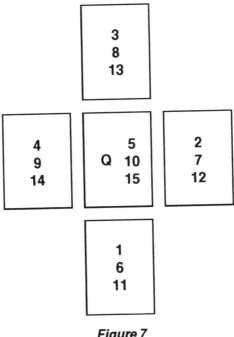

Figure 7

YOUR WISH WITH 32 CARDS

One thing that everyone wants to know is whether a wish will be granted, how soon this will happen and under what circumstances. There are a number of ways of answering questions with the pack of thirty-two cards, and some of the more traditional methods are presented here, together with some of the less familiar ones.

The Questioner is warned that the cards should never be more than once a week when seeking information about a ish.

An Easy Method. The Questioner shuffles the pack of cards and at the same-time concentrates upon his wish, which, however he does not reveal to anyone.

The Seer takes the shuffled pack and deals out nine cards right to left and face down. Then the Seer begins to turn over the cards one at a time, moving from left to right. As soon as he turns up an ace he lays this aside land continues on down the row of cards until he has turned them all face up. If he finds any more aces in the row, he also removes them and places them beside the first ace withdrawn.

He now gathers up the cards which remain in the row and replaces them in the pack, which is reshuffled by the Questioner. The Seer then repeats the process, dealing out nine more cards and hunting for aces. If all the aces have not now appeared, the Seer may repeat the process once more, dealing out a third row of nine cards after the Questioner has thoroughly reshuffled the pack. This must be the last deal, however, and if all the aces have not turned up by the time the third row has been searched, it is a sign that the Questioner will have to work very hard to obtain his wish.

The sooner the aces turn up in the three deals the quicker the wish will be granted. Thus if all four appear in the first row, it is the best possible sign that fulfillment will not be long delayed. This is not a usual circumstance, however, and the Questioner should not be disappointed if it requires three deals to complete the hunt. In such an event it merely indicates that the delay will be longer. If, however, the ace of spades is the first ace to appear, the Questioner is going to be confronted with great obstacles in achieving what he desires.

The Rule of Three. The Questioner begins by deciding which card is to represent him or her, according to the directions given under the heading *General Instructions*. This having been done, the Questioner shuffles the pack thoroughly, keeping the wish fixed in mind. Then the Questioner cuts the pack, and note is taken card which is revealed in the cut. If this card should happen to be the nine of spades, the omen is very unfavorable, and nothing more can be done, for this indicates failure to realize the wish.

In case the cut card is not the nine of spades, the pack is put together again and the Seer deals out the cards into piles. Then he begins to look through each pile in turn to find the card which represents the Questioner. When that is located the other two piles may be discarded.

Now it is necessary to see if the cut card is in the same pile in which the Questioner's card appeared. If it is, this is a sign that the wish will be granted, and the number of cards which turn up between the cut card and the Questioner's card indicate the relative length of time it will take before the wish is granted. Should the nine of spades appear in the same pile with the Questioner's card and the cut card, it is a warning of great difficulty in obtaining the wish. If the nine of spades is not in the pile but more than six other spades are present, this is likewise a warning of trouble to come in connection with the wish.

If the cut card and the Questioner's card do not appear in the same pile, the outcome of the wish is very doubtful, and nothing can be predicted for certain. In this event the Seer , should examine all three piles carefully until the wish card (nine of hearts) has been located. The cards which appear on either side of this - or if it is an end card in a pile, the two cards nearest to it - may provide some message for the Questioner regarding his wish.

The Message of the Aces. From the deck of thirty-two the Seer removes the four aces and places them face down on the table so that the Questioner does not know which ace is which.

The Questioner now shuffles the remaining twenty-eight cards thoroughly, silently concentrating on a wish. The Seer takes the pack and deals out the cards face down into four piles of seven cards each.

Then the Questioner chooses one of the four aces at random and turns it face up. This he places next to one of the four piles of cards. He then selects a second ace, turns it face up and puts it beside another of the four piles. In like manner he turns the two other aces and lays them beside the two remaining piles. Thus each of the four piles of cards is now identified by one of the aces.

The Seer then hunts through each of the four piles in turn he has found the nine of hearts (wish card). If the nine of hearts appears in the pile identified by the ace of spades, it means that the wish will not be granted. If it appears in the of the ace of clubs, the realization of the wish will depend entirely upon how much effort the Questioner puts forth. If he works very hard, he will win his desire very soon. If not, there will be a delay. In other words, it depends entirely upon him.

However, if the wish card appears in the pile of the ace of diamonds, it is a sign that there are factors affecting the realization of the wish over which the Questioner has no control. The card lying near the wish card may give a hint as to whether these factors are favorable or unfavorable. For example, if the ten of hearts lies next to the wish card, this is a sign that regardless of what the Questioner may do, everything will turn out for the best and his wish will be granted without any effort on his part. Or the appearance of the king of clubs would indicate a loyal friend was going to act in the Questioner's interests.

If the wish card appears in the pile of the ace of hearts, it is a sure sign that the wish will be granted speedily and the Questioner will be very happy.

Time Divination. The Questioner hunts through the pack, silently concentrating upon his wish until he finds the wish card (nine of hearts). This he removes and lays on the table before him face down.

Still keeping his thoughts fixed on his wish, the Questioner shuffles the remaining thirty-one cards thoroughly and cuts them into two piles. The Seer removes the top and bottom card of each pile and discards them.

The Questioner places the two piles together again and reshuffles the pack. He now cuts the pack into three piles and the Seer removes only the top card of each one and discards the m.

Now the Questioner gathers up the three piles, shuffles them and cuts them once, without looking at the cut card. The Seer removes this cut card, discards it and puts in its place the new card which has been lying in front of the Questioner. The pack is now joined together once more, and for a last time the Questioner reshuffles, this time thinking intently of his wish.

He gives the pack to the Seer who proceeds to deal out two piles of twelve cards each, face down. This done, the Seer first looks through the left-hand pile. If the wish card is in it, the wish will not come true within a year from the time. However if it is not in this pile, the Seer begins to turn over the cards in the right-hand pile one at a time, counting as he does. The number at which the wish card turns up is the number of months that will elapse before the wish is granted.

THE DECK OF 52 CARDS

When the full deck of fifty-two bridge or playing cards is used for fortune telling, there is no need to mark the cards as is done when only thirty-two are used. In the full pack of fifty-two each card has but a single meaning and no attempt is made to determine whether the card lies in reversed or normal position. As will be seen in the following table, meanings for the full pack differ somewhat from those when only thirty-two cards are used.

THE MEANING OF THE 52 CARDS

CLUBS

ACE - The most favorable card in the deck. Wealth, prosperity, happy and tranquil thoughts.

TWO - Opposition to one's wishes, or a disappointment.

THREE - The Questioner will be married thrice, with wealth in each case.

FOUR - Warning of impending evil, or a change in fortune. i~Wedding, with good prospects for the future.

FIVE - Wedding, with good prospects for the future.

SIX - Hard work in a business, with prosperity as a result.

SEVEN - Good luck, provided someone of the opposite sex doesn't interfere.

EIGHT - Overpowering desire for money, and gambling rabits.

NINE - Unpleasant happenings because of the stubbornness of some person, possibly a friend.

TEN - Wealth obtained unexpectedly.

JACK - A true and reliable friend of either sex.

QUEEN - A charming and affectionate woman, attractive to men.

KING - A man of generous disposition, true in love and very altruistic.

HEARTS

ACE - The house or home of the Questioner.

TWO - Great success, which will be delayed if there are evil cards are near it.

THREE - Warning to the Questioner. There is danger of trouble as a result of lack of caution and prudence.

FOUR - A delayed wedding because of finicky tastes in the choice of a partner.

FIVE - A changeable and jealous nature. Inability to make up one's mind.

SIX - Friendliness and generosity, with a danger of being victimized by unscrupulous persons.

SEVEN - An unreliable, fickle person who may become a foe.

EIGHT - A festive occasion, good food and drink.

NINE - Wish card. It is usually the sign of wealth and position and honor. If surrounded by evil cards, however, it means temporary ruin.

TEN - A favorable omen, which cancels off bad cards near it, and reinforces good ones. It represents generosity and happiness.

JACK - Someone very close to the Questioner, of either sex, such as a wife or husband, a best friend, a sweetheart, etc.

QUEEN - A tactful, lovable, fair-haired woman.

KING - An ardent, well-intentioned man who is more impetuous and hasty than he is wise. Likeable and good natured.

DIAMONDS

ACE - A letter or money, sometimes a ring.

TWO - A love affair.

THREE - Disputes, either in the home (because of some illness or tempered person) or in business (lawsuits and litigation).

FOUR - Trouble and vexations.

FIVE - To a married person this indicates children who will be a source of great joy. Otherwise prosperity in business or sudden tidings.

SIX - Unhappy end to an early marriage. Marrying a second time is to be discouraged.

SEVEN - A large loss connected with material tintings' such as wealth or property.

EIGHT - A wedding occurring late in life. The marriage may not be happy if unfavorable cards are near.

NINE - A surprise having to do with a sum of money. It may be good or bad, depending on surrounding cards.

TEN - Marriage to an individual who was raised in the country. Or a sizeable amount of money.

JACK - A relative or a close acquaintance of the Questioner. Headstrong, stubborn, not altogether loyal or reliable. Beware of his selfishness.

QUEEN - A vivacious vixen, who likes to attract men and has a way with them.

KING - A man whose temper is easily aroused and who is slow to forgive and relentless with those he decides to call enemies.

SPADES

ACE - Some kind of emotional relationship, as a love affair or a friendship, which may bring trouble. See list of Special Combinations.

TWO - A separation of some sort involving a change of place.

THREE - Faithlessness in love, with unhappiness for the Questioner.

FOUR - Envious disposition.

FIVE - Temper leading to quarrels.

SIX - Good plans and intentions meeting with failure.

SEVEN - Loss of a friend or loved one through a quarrel.

EIGHT - Warning of trouble unless the Questioner is very cautious. This may be connected with a difference of opinion with friends or relatives.

Nine - The card of bad luck.

TEN - Misfortunes. This cancels off the good cards next to it.

JACK - A well-meaning acquaintance who will not exert himself to help the Questioner.

QUEEN - A woman who likes scandal and will undertake nefarious business if properly bribed.

KING - A man with a great urge to get ahead in the world.

CARD GROUPS

The meanings of two, three or four of the same kind of card are the same with the pack of fifty-two cards as they are with the reduced pack of thirty-two. Therefore, in reading fortunes with the full pack, refer to the table at the beginning of the section under the heading *Meaning of Card Groups*.

SPECIAL COMBINATIONS WITH 52 CARDS

The following meanings apply only to card combinations which occur when the full pack of fifty-two cards is used. They are presented according to the four suits for rapid identification. It should be understood that these meanings apply only when the cards listed appear side by side.

CLUBS

KING - With the *Ace of Spades*, the King of Clubs represents a man who is active in politics.

EIGHT - With *Ace of Diamonds*, a business offer or proposition.

FOUR - With any *King* or *Queen* the four of clubs indicates that the person referred to by the King or Queen is going to suffer an injustice. With any *Jack* it indicates that the person referred to by that Jack is going to lose something.

TWO - With *two of diamonds*, an unexpected message.

HEARTS

ACE - When a heart card appears beside the Ace, a friendship is indicated. When hearts appear on both sides of the Ace, it indicates a love affair. When the Ace has diamonds on either side of it, money is indicated. When the Ace has spades on either side of it, quarrels are indicated.

NINE - With *five of spades*, loss of social position

EIGHT - With *five of hearts*, a gift of jewelry.

FIVE - With *eight of diamonds*, a gift of money. With *eight of hearts*, a gift of jewelry.

FOUR - With any *King* or *Queen* the four of hearts indicates that the person referred to by the King or Queen has had a number of love affairs. With any *Jack*, it indicates that the person referred to by that Jack is going to marry presently. With the *Ace of Spades*, a child is to be born.

TWO - With *ten of diamonds*, a marriage bringing wealth.

DIAMONDS

ACE - With *eight of clubs*, a business offer or proposition.

TEN - With *two of hearts*, a marriage bringing wealth.

NINE - With any *King or Queen* the nine of diamonds indicates that the person referred to by the King or Queen will never realize complete success because of an inability to concentrate. With any *Jack* it means that the person referred to by that Jack is going to be made unhappy through his own actions. With the *eight of spades*, a bitter quarrel with a friend who has turned enemy.

EIGHT - With *five of hearts*, a gift of money.

SEVEN - With *nine of spades*, loss of money.

TWO - With two *of clubs*, an unexpected message.

SPADES

ACE - With *King of Clubs* the Ace of Spades indicates that the King of Clubs is a man who is active in politics. With *ten of spades*, a serious undertaking. With *four of hearts*, a child is to be born.

TEN - When a *club* card appears beside the ten of spades, trouble in business is indicated. When *clubs* appear on both sides of the ten, it indicates a grave business loss through theft, forgery or mismanagement.

NINE - With *seven of diamonds*, loss of money.

EIGHT - With *nine of diamonds*, a bitter quarrel with a friend who has turned enemy. If the eight appears next to the Questioner's card, he should be warned to abandon whatever plans he is now making.

FIVE - With *nine of hearts*, loss of social position.

THE SQUARE OF NINE

From the full pack of fifty-two cards the Questioner chooses one to represent himself according to the rules given under the heading *General Instructions*. The remaining fifty-one are now carefully shuffled and cut with the left hand into two packs. The Seer removes the bottom of each of the packs and discards it. The Questioner joins the two packs and shuffles them once more.

Seer takes the cards and proceeds to deal out in a row three packs of five cards each. This done he lays the next card aside face down as part of the Surprise. He now deals off a second row directly beneath the first one and likewise containing three packs of five cards each. Again he lays aside a card face down for the Surprise. He deals out three more packs of five cards each in a third row which is placed directly beneath the second row. He now has a square formed of nine packs each containing five cards (See Fig. 8).

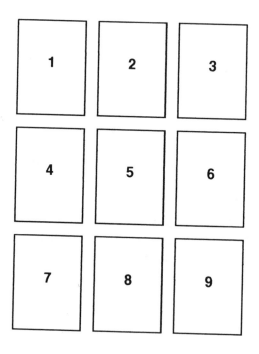

Figure 8

There remain in the Seer's hand two cards. The top one he.lays aside in the Surprise face down. The other one, which is known as the Indicator, he lays face up before him. If the Indicator is a heart, the Seer picks up the packs numbered 1, 5 and 9 in the diagram and discards the other packs. If the Indicator is a club, the Seer picks up packs 3, 5 and 7, discarding the rest. If the Indicator is a diamond, the Seer picks up packs 4, 7 and 8 and throws away the others. If it is a spade, he picks up packs 2, 3 and 6, discarding the rest.

In any case the Questioner's card which was previously chosen is now added to the three packs which have been picked up, and these sixteen cards are shuffled by the Questioner. The Seer then deals them out in a row on the table and proceeds to study their message. When this has been done, he turns over the three cards in the Surprise to ascertain what unexpected happening is going to affect the success and happiness of the Questioner. It should be remembered that in this method the meanings given for the full pack of fifty-two cards are to be used by the Seer.

THE SEVEN PACKS

The Questioner shuffles the cards carefully and cuts the into three packs. The Seer picks up the center pack and places it on top of the one on the left. These he then places on top of the one which was on the right. Now the Seer deals off the top card, face down, and says aloud, "What was." The second card is dealt off and laid face down to the right of the first card the Seer saying aloud, "What will be." The third card is laid down in the row with the words, "To you." The fourth is placed face down to the right of the third with the words, "To your best beloved." The fifth is laid down in the row with the words, "Your house." The sixth, placed next to the fifth, is designated with the words, "What you hope for." The seventh and last in the row is laid down with the words, "A surprise."

With the row of seven cards now established, the Seer proceeds to deal off a second row of cards on top of the first seven, always moving from left to right, and this process is continued until the entire pack has been dealt off. There are now seven piles of cards and it will be noted that the first three piles on the left contain eight cards, while the remaining four contain only seven.

The Seer now spreads out the cards in the first pack on the left, "What was", and proceeds to read their message, which naturally refers to the Questioner's past. In spreading out the pack, the Seer does so by first turning it face up and then dealing off the cards one at a time in a row from left to right. The message is likewise read from left to right, the meaning of the first card on the left being linked to the meaning of the second card, and so on, as has been illustrated in the model reading given in the earlier.

The messages of the other six packs are read in turn. The second pack, "What will be," refers to the Questioner's future; the third,

"To you," to the Questioner himself at the present moment. The fourth refers to the Questioner's sweetheart, the fifth to his house, and the sixth to his wish. The last pack contains a message of a surprise which will unexpectedly affect his fortunes.

THE FIVE MESSAGES

In reality this is but a variation of the preceding method, but it is preferred by some students of cards. The full pack of fifty-two cards is thoroughly shuffled by the Questioner, who then cuts it with the left hand into two piles. The Seer removes the top card of the pile on the left and the bottom card of the pile on the right, and the Questioner then rejoins the cards and reshuffles them.

The Seer now deals off four cards and then takes the fifth and discards it. He deals off four more and again discards the fifth. This process is continued until the entire pack has been dealt off. Now the cards are once more shuffled by the Questioner and then handed to the Seer who proceeds to deal off five in a row face down and left to right. A second row is laid down on top of the first five and so on until all cards have been dealt out into the five packs, which are known - from left to right - as "The Heart," "The Home," "The Hope," "The Head" and "The Surprise."

Taking the first pack on the left - "The Heart" - the Seer turns it face up and deals off the cards one at a time from left to right in a row. Their message refers to the Questioner's sweetheart. The next pack - "The Home" - is similarly dealt out and read, and it naturally refers to the Questioner's home. The third or "Hope" pack refers to the Questioner's wish; the "Head" pack refers to the Questioner himself at the present and the last pack concerns the unexpected event which will affect his future happiness and success.

QUESTIONING THE CARDS

The Questioner first chooses a card to represent himself according to the rules given under heading *General Instructions*. This is laid in the center of the table face up. The remaining fifty-one cards are now thoroughly shuffled by the Questioner, who cuts the pack with the left hand into two piles of approximately equal size. The Seer takes the left-hand pack and from it deals off nine cards in a circle around the Questioner's card and face down. The Seer now joins the right- hand pack with the cards which remain in his hand and gives them to the

Questioner, who shuffles them again.

This time there is no cut and the Seer takes the pack from the Questioner and proceeds to deal off a second circle around the first one. The second circle contains eighteen cards face down. The cards which remain in the Seer's hand are once more shuffled by the Questioner, after which the Seer takes them and deals all of them off in a third circle, face down and outside the two smaller circles.

There are now nine cards in the small circle, eighteen in the middle circle and twenty-four in the outer one. The Questioner now slowly turns over fifteen cards - selecting them at random and as each card is turned face up the Seer reads its meaning, noting the connection which it has with the preceding card and the one which is turned up after it. In this way the Questioner picks out himself the message which lies waiting for him in the triple circle of cards.

THE THREE ANSWERS

The Questioner chooses three subjects about which he wants forecasts. A card is chosen to represent each of these subjects. Customary subjects and the cards which represent them are: *the home* - Ace of Hearts; *the wish*—nine of hearts; *business* - six of clubs; *the wedding* - five of clubs; *success in the future* - two of hearts; *Happiness in the future* - ten of hearts; *the love affair* - two of diamonds; *words of warning* - three of hearts.

Let us suppose the Questioner wishes to learn what the future holds for him in regard to his love affair, his business and his home. From the pack of fifty-two cards he removes the two of diamonds, the six of clubs and the ace of hearts. These three Indicators he lays face down upon the table and the Seer mixes them up until the Questioner no longer remembers which is which.

Now the Questioner takes the remaining cards and shuffles them carefully. The Seer takes the pack and proceeds to deal out in a row seven piles of seven cards each, dealing from right to left. This done, the Seer takes the third and fifth piles and discards them. The remaining cards are gathered together and reshuffled by the Questioner, who then cuts them into three packs.

From the center pack the Seer removes the top card and discards it. From each of the two other packs the Seer removes the top and bottom cards and discards them. The remaining cards are now once more shuffled by the Questioner. Then the Seer proceeds to deal them out - right to left - into three piles.

Now the Questioner selects one of the Indicator cards, which are lying face down, of course, and places it above the center pile of cards. The other two Indicator cards he places above the remaining two piles in whichever order he chooses.

The Seer now turns over the Indicator card which is above the pile on the left. If this should happen to be the two of diamonds, it means that this pile of cards contains the message relating to the Questioner's love affair. The Seer deals off the cards from this pile in a row, moving from right to left, and proceeds to read the message, reading from *left to right*.

In like manner the Indicator above the center pile is turned face up to show the nature of the message in the center pile, and those cards are read in the same manner. So, also, the message contained in the remaining pile is studied.

THE FOUR STARS

The Questioner chooses four subjects about which he wishes to obtain forecasts, removing from the pack of fifty-two the four cards appropriate to these subjects, as has been described in the preceding section. These four Indicator cards are laid out on the table face up, allowing plenty of space around each card.

The remaining cards in the pack are now shuffled by the Questioner and handed to the Seer. Choosing any one of the four Indicator cards at random, the Seer deals off three cards from the pack and places them beside it in a pile, face down. He now picks a second Indicator card and deals off beside it three more cards face down. The same is done for the third and fourth Indicators. Returning to the first Indicator, he deals off three more; then three for the second Indicator and so on. This process is continued until all the cards have been dealt out

Now taking the pile of cards beside the first Indicator, the Seer proceeds to lay them out around the Indicator as follows: the first is placed face up above the Indicator, the second face up below it and to the left, the third face up below it and to the right. The fourth goes above the first, the fifth below and to the left of the second, and so on as is illustrated in Fig. 9 in which the card marked I stands for the Indicator.

In similar fashion a star is built up about the second Indicator from its pile of cards, and about the third and fourth Indicators from their piles of cards.

Now taking the first Indicator, the Seer reads off the messages of the cards. If the Indicator card happens to be the ace of hearts, the Seer notes the message regarding the Questioner's home which is contained in the top point of the star. This is composed of cards 10, 7, 4 and 1; then the message in the left point (cards 11, 8, 5 and 2), and finally the one in the right point (cards 12, 9, 6 and 3). The cards are usually read inward, from the end of the point toward the Indicator card.

When the messages of the three points of the star have been read, the twelve cards are gathered together, shuffled by the Questioner and then dealt out in a row by the Seer, who proceeds to read the meaning of the entire twelve, starting from the left. The Seer should remember to note ball the meanings of groups of cards and all special combinations.

In similar fashion the cards about each of the three other Indicators are read.

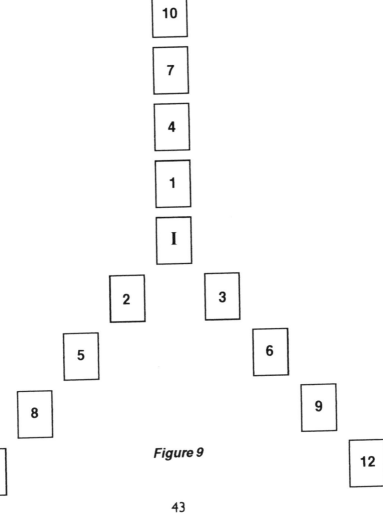

Figure 9

THE EGYPTIAN PYRAMID

The Questioner shuffles the pack thoroughly and cuts it into three piles with the left hand. The Seer removes the top and bottom card of each pile and discards them. The Questioner reshuffles the cards and cuts them into two packs. From these the Seer removes the top and bottom cards and likewise discards them. The pack is shuffled a third time by the Question and handed to the Seer.

The Seer deals off a row of six cards right to left and face up, spacing them rather wide apart. He then deals off six more cards and discards them. Now he deals off a second row of five cards *left to right* and face down, placing them above the row of six, as is indicated in Fig. 10. (The arrows in each row show in which direction the deal is made.) After the second row is dealt off, he discards five cards.

The third row, of four cards, is placed above the second and is dealt *right to left*. After this four cards are dealt off and discarded. Next a row of three cards is dealt above this *left to right,* and then three cards are discarded. Two cards are then dealt off above and *right to left*. The next two cards are not discarded, however, but are laid aside face down for the Surprise. One more card is dealt out to form the top of the pyramid, and the card which remains in the Seer's hand is added to the Surprise, face down.

The Seer now proceeds to read the message of the pyramid starting with the top card and proceeding down through the rows, first right to left, then left to right, as is indicated by the arrows at the ends of the rows in Fig. 10.

Care should be taken to note the meaning of any groups special combinations which appear in the pyramid. Since each row is considered to be continuous with the row on either side of it, the possibility of special combinations in the end cards should not be overlooked. Thus in Fig. 10 if the card labeled **A** should happen to be the *eight of clubs* and the card labeled **B** should be the *ace of diamonds*, they would be considered a combination (representing a business proposition), since the reading proceeds from left to right along the row of three cards and continues without break from right to left along the row of four cards.

It is considered a very good sign if the nine of hearts (wish card) appears in the pyramid. If it is found in the bottom row it is a sign that the Questioner's wish will be granted within a very short space of time. If it should happen to be the top card, then the Questioner is sure to have his wish come true and to receive even more than he had hoped for.

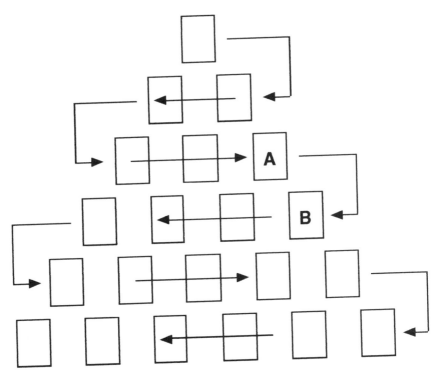

Figure 10

Likewise if the five of clubs appears in either the row of three or four cards, it is an indication that the Questioner will be involved in a wedding, though he may not necessarily be the one who is to be married. The ten of hearts appearing in the row of two or of three cards is a sign of great happiness to come and cancels off much of the misfortune which other unfavorable cards in the pyramid may portend.

If however, the three of hearts or the eight of spades should be in the row of two or of three cards, the Questioner should very cautious about proceeding with any of his plans. If either of these happens to be the top card, it is a warning to be heeded.

AN OLD-COUNTRY METHOD

A method which is often used among European fortune tellers is as follows: The Questioner chooses a card to represent himself according to the directions given under the heading *General Instructions*. He then shuffles the full pack of fifty-two cards and cuts them in four packs. The Seer takes the pack on the right and puts it on top of the pack second from the left. These he places on top of the one which is on the left. Now the remaining pack is placed on top of these. The whole pack is spread out by the Seer face down on the table and the Questioner chooses seventeen cards at random and, without looking them, hands them to the Seer. The rest of the pack is the taken up and laid aside temporarily. Taking the seventeen cards, the Seer proceeds to deal them out face up in the form of a cross, following the order which is indicated in Fig. 11. Special note is taken of any groups a special combinations.

If the Questioner's card is among these seventeen, it is a very lucky sign. However, aces detract from this good luck according to the number of them present. If one ace appears as well as the Questioner's card, the luck will not last very long. If two aces appear together with the Questioner's card, there will a long delay before the lucky break occurs. If three or four aces appear in addition to the Questioner's card, the good luck is practically canceled off.

If the nine of hearts appears in either of the side branches the wish will be granted. If it appears in the upper branch of the cross, there will be a delay. If it appears in the lower branch, there will be obstacles hindering its realization.

Kings bring luck for a feminine Questioner, queens for a masculine one. The jacks of hearts and diamonds portend success and happiness, the jacks of spades and clubs are warnings of loss or failure.

The upper and lower branch should be read together, that is, the message should be traced by starting with card No. 13 and proceeding on down through 12, 11, 10, 1, 14, 15, 16 and 17.

The side branches are considered as having separate messages, one being contained in cards 5, 4, 3, and 2; the other in cards 9, 8, 7 and 6, in that order. The latter group in some instances is regarded as containing the Surprise.

Whatever card appears in the center of the cross, that is, in position No. 1, is regarded as being especially significant. It should also be noted that even-numbered cards in the cross are lucky for women, odd- numbered ones for men. The odd-numbered ones are bad for women, the even-numbered unlucky for men.

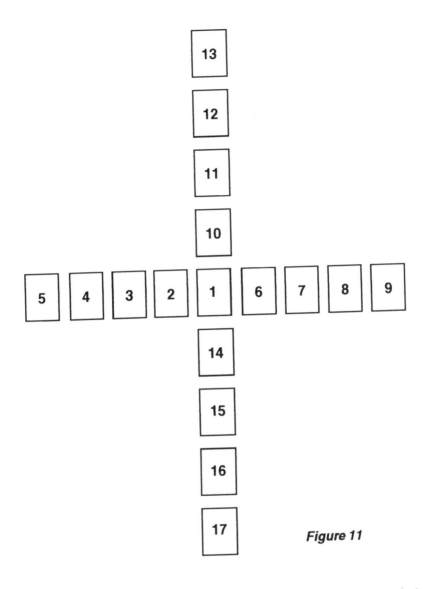

Figure 11

When the meanings of the cards have been completely analyzed, the seventeen are laid aside. The remainder of the pack is now shuffled by the Questioner and cut with the left hand. The Seer takes the cut card and without looking at it places it face down on the table before him. Now from each of the two piles into which the cards have been cut by the Questioner the Seer takes the first four top cards. These, together with the cut card, total nine, and they are shuffled by the Questioner. The rest of the pack is discarded.

The Seer now deals out the nine cards face up to form the figure illustrated in Fig. 12, the numbers indicating the order in which the cards are laid down.

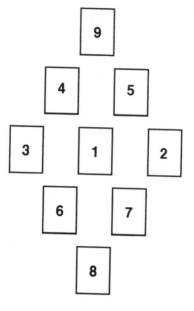

Figure 12

If the Questioner's card should happen to be among these nine, it is also a very lucky sign, though as before the aces detract from such a fortunate occurrence. Care should be taken to note any special combinations or groups. The card which is found in position 1 is of greatest importance. It is not considered lucky if any one of the jacks is found in position 2 or 3. The meaning of the cards is determined by reading them in sequence, starting with the top one, 9, and proceeding as follows: 4, 5, 3, 1, 2, 6, 7 and 8. It is a good sign if clubs or diamonds are found in positions 4, 5, 6 and 7. Spades in these positions are unlucky.

YOUR WISH WITH 52 CARDS

In addition to the methods of answering wish questions with the selected pack of thirty-two cards there are a number of ways to do this with the full pack of fifty-two. In summarizing these, it should be emphasized that none of these methods should be consulted more than once a week.

The Twelve Months. The Questioner first chooses a card to represent himself according to the directions given at under the heading *General Instructions*. This is laid face up in the center of the table. The remaining fifty-one cards are then thoroughly shuffled by the Questioner.

The Seer takes the pack and proceeds to lay out a circle of twelve cards around the Questioner's card as follows:

To the right of the Questioner's card he lays the first card face down. To the left of the Questioner's card he places the second card face down. The third card is placed above the Questioner's card and the fourth below it. In Fig. 13 is indicated the order in which the cards are placed. As can be seen by consulting this diagram, the fifth and sixth cards are arranged in a curve between card No. 1 and card No. 3. In the same manner the seventh and eighth cards are laid down between card No. 3 and card No. 2, and so on until the circle of twelve has been completed.

The Seer now takes the thirteenth card and lays it to one side face down to form part of the Surprise. After this is done the rest of the pack is handed to the Questioner who shuffles it.

The Seer then takes the pack and deals off twelve more cards, laying them in the same order as before face down on top of the first circle of twelve cards. When this has been done the next card in the pack is likewise laid to one side in the Surprise.

Again the Questioner shuffles the remaining cards in the pack for a last time and the Seer then deals them off around the circle for a fourth time.

We now have twelve piles of four cards each lying around the Questioner's card. The pile which is numbered 3 in Fig. 13 stands for the month of January. Pile No. 7 is February, pile No. 8 is March, pile No. 2 is April and so on around the circle to pile No. 6, which is December. Beginning with January, the Seer turns over the cards in each pile until he locates the nine of hearts. The pile in which this card is found stands for the month within the coming twelve months during which Questioner's wish will come true.

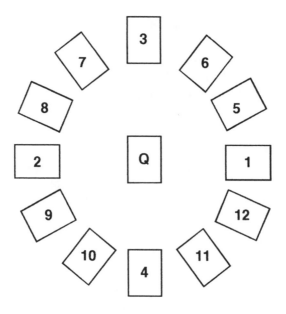

Figure 13

The three cards in the Surprise are now turned over and studied to discover what unexpected set of circumstances will lead to the realization of the Questioner's wish.

If it should happen that the nine of hearts is not to be fount in any of the month-piles, it is a sign that there is no certainty that the wish will come true. The nine of hearts will be found in the Surprise, and the other two cards in the Surprise will indicate factors over which the Questioner has no control which may prevent him from realizing what he is hoping for.

The Aztec Star. The Questioner first chooses a card to represent himself according to the rules given under the heading *General Instructions*. This is laid aside temporarily while the remaining cards are carefully shuffled by the Questioner, who must keep his mind fixed on his wish while doing so and must not tell it to anyone. The Questioner cuts the cards and then hands them to the Seer.

The Seer deals off four cards face down on the table so as to form a good-sized square. The order in which these are laid down is indicated in Fig. 14, the first card going in the upper right corner, the second in the upper left, the third in the lower right, and so forth. The

Questioner's card is now placed face up in the center of this square, as indicated in the diagram. The Seer now lays the fifth card face down above the square and the sixth face down below it. (See Pig. 14.) The Star has now been completed.

The Questioner takes the pack from the Seer, reshuffles it and cuts it into two piles. The Seer removes the top card of the left-hand pile and the bottom card of the right-hand pile and lays them aside as the Surprise. Then the Seer puts the left hand pile on top of the right hand pile and proceeds to deal off the cards face down onto the ones which form the Star, following this order:

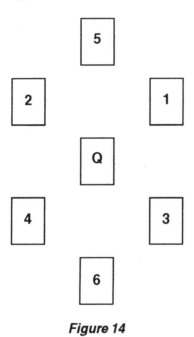

Figure 14

First he puts one on the Questioner's , then one on card No. 1, another on card No. 2, another on card No. 3, the next on No. 4, the next on No. 5 and the next on No. 6. After that another on the Questioner's card, then the next on No. 1, and so on until the entire pack has been dealt off.

Now the Seer examines the seven cards which are piled on top of the Questioner's card. If the nine of hearts happens to be among them, it is a very favorable sign and indicates that the Questioner's wish will be granted very speedily. If it is not in that pile, he then examines the other piles of cards until he finds it. If the nine of hearts is in the pile on card

No. 1, it a sign that there will be a long delay before the wish is granted. If it is in pile No. 2, the wish will be granted but there will trouble coming as a result of it. If it is in No. 3, the Questioner will not get his wish unless he is prepared to work very hard to obtain it. If it is in No. 4, he will have to be on guard again enemies who will do everything in their power to prevent him from obtaining his wish. If it is in No. 5, the wish will not be granted until the Questioner has mended a quarrel in which he has been involved, or is going to get into. If it is in No. 6, the wish will be realized as the result of some kind action on the part of the Questioner's friends or acquaintances.

If the nine of hearts is in none of these piles, it is very unlikely that the wish will be granted. The card will be found in the Surprise, and the other card with it will give a clue as to the factor which will operate to prevent the realization of the wish.

THE TEN PACKS

The Questioner shuffles the full pack of fifty-two cards. The Seer deals off a row of ten cards face down and then deals second row of ten face down on top of them. He then lays the next card aside as part of the Surprise and proceeds to deal them ten more on top of the row. The cards remaining in his hand are now spread out face down on the table and the Questioner selects two at random and lays them face down for the Surprise. The remaining cards are again shuffled by the Questioner and then the Seer proceeds to deal them out on the row of ten until he has run out of cards. It will be noticed that there are now ten packs of cards, but one of them will contain only four instead of five cards.

If this pack of four cards should contain the nine of hearts the wish will not be granted. If the nine of hearts appears in any of the other nine packs, the cards which lie next to it should be examined carefully. If the card which represents the Questioner according to the rules given under the heading *General Instructions*, should lie next to the nine of hearts, the wish will be granted speedily. Otherwise there may be some delay, the nature of which will be indicated by the cards which surround the nine of hearts.

If it appears in none of these ten packs, then it is in the Surprise, and the other two cards in that pile will give a hint as to how the wish will be granted. When the nine of hearts turns up in the Surprise, it indicates that some unforeseen event is going to affect the wish.

New Revised

The Master Book of Candle Burning

How to Burn Candles for Every Purpose

POWERFUL **PSALM** RITUALS

HENRI GAMACHE

#043
$7.95

"How can I burn candles in a manner which will bring me the most satisfaction and consolation?"

In order to answer that question it is necessary to eliminate all technical, dry and often times torturous historical background. It is necessary to sift and sort every fact, scrutinize every detail, search for the kernel.

It is to be hoped that this volume answers that question in a manner which is satisfactory to the reader. It has been necessary, of course, to include some historical data and other anthropological data in order to better illustrate the symbolism involved in modern candle burning as practiced by so many people today.

This data has been accumulated from many sources: it has been culled from literally hundreds of books and articles. The modern rituals outlined here are based upon practices which have been described by mediums, spiritual advisors, evangelists, religious interpreters and others who should be in a position to know.

It has been the author's desire to interpret and explain the basic symbolism involved in a few typical exercises so that the reader may recognize this symbolism and proceed to develop his own symbolism in accordance with the great beauty and highest ethics of the Art.

ISBN 0-942272-56-0 5½"x 8½" $7.95

ITEM #065

$5.95

Unhexing and Jinx Removing

By Donna Rose

Everywhere we turn these days it seems as if there are forces working against us. You don't need to spend your time thinking, worrying about or stressing over the evils that are constantly prowling. Cast out all forces of negativity, evil thoughts, evil intentions, evil spirits and so on. Break up conspiracies, dispel rumors, blanket your enemies with suffering and confusion. Believe it or not there are ways to protect yourself in this modern world. The easy to perform rituals and spells provided in this book will allow you to escape the dangers hounding you.

ISBN 0-942272-84-6 5½"x 8½" $5.95

ITEM #172

$8.95

HELPING YOURSELF WITH
MAGICKAL OILS A-Z

BY MARIA SOLOMON

The most thorough and comprehensive
workbook available on the

Magickal Powers of
Over 1000 Oils!

Easy to follow step-by-step instructions
*for more than 1500
Spells, Recipes and Rituals for*
Love, Money, Luck, Protection
and much more!

ISBN 0-942272-49-8 5½"x 8½" $8.95

TOLL FREE: 1 (888) OCCULT - 1

ITEM #421
$6.95

PROTECTION
SPELLS & CHARMS

BY JADE

PROTECT YOUR RELATIONSHIP
PROTECT YOUR MATE
PROTECTION AGAINST SLANDER
REMOVE A CURSE
PREVENT UNWANTED VISITORS
PROTECTION FROM INJURY
ROSE OF JERICO
PROTECT AGAINST POSSESSION
PROTECT FROM VIOLENT CRIME

PROTECT YOUR PROPERTY
PREVENT ACCIDENTS
HOUSE BLESSING
COURT SPELLS
PROTECT YOUR CHILDREN
CHANGE A BAD SITUATION
RETURN EVIL
DISCOVER ENEMIES
BANISH ILLNESS

TOLL FREE: 1 (888) OCCULT - 1

ITEM #089
$6.95

MONEY MAGIC

By Jade

NO DESIRE IS BEYOND YOUR REACH!
NO SECRET LONGING IS UNATTAINABLE!

Money and How to Get It
Wealth and Prosperity
Gambling and Games of Chance
Jobs & Promotions
Success in Business
Overcome Financial Problems

**PAPA JIM'S
HERBAL MAGIC
WORKBOOK**

HOW TO USE HERBS FOR
MAGICAL PURPOSES
AN A-Z GUIDE

**ITEM #053
$7.95**

PAPA JIM'S
HERBAL MAGIC
WORKBOOK

Papa Jim is a very famous healer and root doctor. He brings you this compilation of remedies and potions from all over the world. Share the secret recipes that have mystically solved the problems of Papa Jim's many devotees. Learn how to unleash the magical powers of herbs.

Follow easy instructions on how to make
Herbal Baths, Mojo Bags, Sprinkling Powders,
Incenses and Teas for Love, Luck, Sex,
Money Drawing, Gambling
Protection, Hex Breaking, Jinx Removing and more!

Also incudes
English to Spanish / Spanish to English
translation for over 150 common herbs!

ISBN 0-942272-64-1 5½"x 8½" 112 pages $7.95

TOLL FREE: 1 (888) OCCULT - 1

ITEM #224
$5.95

Revised and Expanded

Success and Power Through Psalms

By Donna Rose

For thousands of years, men and women have found in the Psalms the perfect prayer book, possessing wisdom applicable to every human situation. Wise men and women of deep mystical insight have also learned to decipher the magical formulas David and the other Psalmists hid behind the written words. These formulas help the seeker solve everyday problems, achieve higher states of consciousness, gain material and spiritual wealth, as well as help defend himself or herself against psychic attacks and all manner of dangers.

The Revised and Expanded edition of Donna Rose's classic offers over 300 simple to perform magical rituals to help you manifest all of your desires using the magical powers of the psalms.

ISBN 0-942272-79-X 5½"x 8½ $5.95